FRESH
EXPRESSIONS
OF
CHURCH

FRESH EXPRESSIONS OF CHURCH

Travis Collins

Scripture quotations, unless otherwise indicated, are taken
from the Holy Bible, New International Version®, NIV®
Copyright © 1973, 1978, 1984, 2011 by Biblica, Inc.™
Used by permission. All rights reserved worldwide.

Scripture quotations marked THE MESSAGE are taken
from The Message Copyright © by Eugene H.
Peterson 1993, 1994, 1995, 1996, 2000, 2001, 2002.
Used by permission of NavPress Publishing Group.

Printed in the United States of America

Paperback ISBN: 978-1-62824-251-5
Mobi ISBN: 978-1-62824-252-2
ePub ISBN: 978-1-62824-253-9
uPDF ISBN: 978-1-62824-254-6

Library of Congress Control Number: 2015949509

Cover design by Nikabrik Design
Page design by PerfecType

SEEDBED PUBLISHING
Franklin, Tennessee
www.seedbed.com
SOW FOR A GREAT AWAKENING

CONTENTS

PART 1 A TRANSFORMATIONAL MOVEMENT

Many reading this will have looked around the sanctuary or worship center and noted that the congregation is getting smaller and older. It's true in churches across North America. Many people are just not interested in being a part of the congregations that those of us who grew up in church love so deeply.

Some people are hostile toward the church because they've been disappointed, angered, or shamed by church people. Many others are simply indifferent toward the church. They might send their children to the local church's preschool. They might play basketball on open nights in the church's gymnasium. They might even ask to rent the sanctuary for their daughter's wedding. Actually becoming part of the local church's life, however, is of little interest to growing millions of people.

Hence all the statistics you keep hearing about plummeting church attendance, congregations closing their doors, and so on. Moreover, lots of those who are far from church are far from God. The 2015 Pew Research stated that the percentage of Americans who describe themselves as Christians fell about 8 points—from 78.4 to 70.6 percent—between 2007 and 2014. Furthermore, missiologist Alan Hirsch suggested that only 40 to 50 percent of the American population is reachable by church as we know it, and he believes that number is decreasing.[1] That means 50 to 60 percent of the people around us are not going to come to our churches as we know them no matter how well we do things.

For some, this trend is essentially puzzling and annoying. For others, however, the trend is absolutely heartbreaking. For people who hurt for those who are far from God, something deep within them longs to make a difference. For those who believe in God's mission, and the place the church has in that mission, the crumbling of the church in North America is agonizing.

This is where fresh expressions (new forms) of church enter the picture. These fresh expressions of church are right now being used by God's Spirit to engage people who seem unlikely ever to connect with church in its current form. Alongside present congregations there are innovative expressions of the body of Christ that are reaching people that many churches want to reach but simply cannot. Beside tall-steeple churches there are creative, often small, simple groups—fresh expressions of church—through which people are finding their way to faith in Jesus. The stories of genuine, often dramatic, life transformation through these innovative faith communities are nothing less than remarkable.

These leading-edge types of church are now found in multiple countries, in almost countless settings, and among various traditions and denominations. God is blessing these fresh expressions of church with transformed lives, and the movement is helping established congregations find new ways to invest themselves in God's mission to a changing world.

Families are being salvaged, individuals and those who love them are being rescued from the demons of addiction, and people are finding their part in God's mission to the world. Nominal Christians are becoming fully devoted followers of Jesus. People are experiencing a transformation so radical that Jesus called it a "new birth." Fresh expressions of church offer real hope for the future of the Christian faith, and real hope for people who need Jesus and his church.

WHAT IS A FRESH EXPRESSION OF CHURCH?

From the monks to the Mennonites, from the Waldensians to the Wesleyans, from the Pietists to the Pentecostals, God has often raised up people who love him, who love those who are far from him, and who have been willing to be "church" differently for the sake of a thrilling mission. This international, multidenominational, evangelical, missional movement called Fresh Expressions has emerged as a new enterprise with a great heritage.

A fresh expression, simply put, is a new form of church for the new world in which we live. The phrase grew out of a pledge within the ordination vows of the Church of England to "proclaim the Gospel afresh in every generation."[2] A widely accepted definition of a fresh expression of church came from the joint work of the Church of England and the British Methodist Church in 2006:

A fresh expression is a form of church for our changing culture established primarily for the benefit of people who are not yet members of any church.

- *It will come into being through principles of listening, service, incarnational mission, and making disciples.*
- *It will have the potential to become a mature expression of church shaped by the gospel and the enduring marks of the church and for its cultural context.*[3]

A fresh expression of church is not something temporary, like a mission trip or an annual sporting event that simply gathers people together. It is not a tweak of the present form of church, like a new worship service. It's not an arm of a present church, like a food pantry. It's not a new name for a revamped, long-standing ministry. And it's not merely a step toward a church. It's more than all these things.

A fresh expression of church is a *church*, and is characterized by the elements and enduring marks of a church: it is *up*, *out*, *in*, and *of*. Meaning there is an *up*ward reach toward God, an *out*ward reach to people beyond our circle, an *in*ward commitment to discipleship and fellowship, and a clear understanding that the church is part *of* the universal church and part of a deep, historical stream. Fresh expressions of church take their place as part of the one, holy, catholic (universal), and apostolic church.

A fresh expression of church is . . .

- gathered around the resurrected Christ;
- primarily for those who are not likely to engage with an established church;
- an ongoing community;
- attentive to a subculture, a particular population group—i.e., a group of people who share a similar interest, hobby, need, community, or work;
- outside the traditions and usually outside the walls of established churches;
- contextualized, indigenous, fitting the local context;
- probably smaller-scale than what we tend to think of for new churches; and
- intended to engage people who are far from God.

The following description is found often in Fresh Expressions literature from the United Kingdom. Fresh expressions of church are . . .

- *Missional*—They are intended to join God in his loving efforts to reach people who are unchurched and far from God; fresh expressions are sometimes referred to as "witnessing communities."

- *Contextual*—They fit, occur naturally within, the given context.
- *Formational*—From the beginning they have discipleship—the formation of disciples—as their aim.
- *Ecclesial*—In their mature stages they are fully church, not a step toward, or a substitute for, church.[4]

A fresh expression of church is a Jesus-centered community of faith among people who are willing to practice a new way of life but perhaps never would have come to our church buildings. Of course a fresh expression could grow out of the desires of devoted Christ-followers who want to experience church in a way more meaningful to them than existing congregations can offer. The movement is rooted, however, in a passion for those far from God and from his church.

RETHINKING FORMS OF CHURCH

Fresh expressions of church compel us to reconsider our notion of church. I was having lunch with Jay and Lisa Smith, leaders of a fresh expression among the arts community near Washington, DC, when Lisa asked a great question: "How much of what we *call* church are we willing to give up in order to *be* church?" We will need to force ourselves out of the unnecessarily stereotypical and restrictive categories we often associate with church if we are going to make disciples of all people, not just the ones who are open to churches as they now look and function.

Fresh expressions give us permission to rethink the day and time of our worship gatherings, who leads or facilitates, the location and size of meeting space, our expectations of numerical success, and what membership means. Unlike some church-planting efforts, a fresh expression of church is not going to replicate the mother church, and usually will not begin with a worship service or Bible study. Also, fresh expressions tend to be even more likely than typical new church plants to engage people who have no history with, or attraction to, church.

Whether or not a denominational agency recognizes this new form as a proper church will depend on criteria unique to each body.

In the beginning, some denominations might struggle to find a category in which to place these new expressions of church. One key to the future of fresh expressions of church is the creative willingness of denominational bodies to bless and recognize them as fully church.

A "MIXED ECONOMY"

We are witnessing an emerging partnership between churches that have been around for a long time and new churches that look very different. In England, where this movement began, leaders speak of "the mixed economy of church," reminding us that church today needs both inherited and fresh approaches.

So, is there truly an ongoing place for a local church with a steeple, the 11:00 a.m. Sunday morning worship service, and all those committees? Absolutely, there is! That congregation has been making a difference in the lives of its people, and in its community, for decades. It has an identity that is inimitable and an influence that is irreplaceable. It is at the heart of God's mission to the world. God's Spirit is alive and well in present churches of all ages, shapes, and sizes.

So the movement called Fresh Expressions is about new forms of church *coming alongside* (not replacing) existing congregations. Members of those existing churches (sometimes called "inherited churches") often are the ones who launch these new forms of church. Their ministers often mentor the pioneers who lead fresh expressions of church. Some congregations actually provide funding or meeting space for fresh expressions.

Some of these new forms of church are formed independently, by pioneers, without the assistance of existing congregations. Yet, however they begin, fresh expressions of church rely on the traditions of inherited churches as important starting points, or frameworks, for how they will "be church" in a new way.

HOW DID IT ALL GET STARTED?

The Fresh Expressions movement was born in England. The term "fresh expressions of church" first appeared in an Anglican paper titled *Mission-Shaped Church* in

2004.[5] Those on the study team that pro-
duced *Mission-Shaped Church* became
increasingly aware of something happening
around them—new forms of church were
reaching people the inherited church was
not reaching. Thus the researchers uncov-
ered, recognized, reviewed, blessed, and
encouraged what we now know as *fresh
expressions of church*. A year after the pub-
lication of that watershed document, the
network/movement/initiative called Fresh
Expressions was born.

British Methodists, then others, joined
in the effort and now numerous Christian
groups in England are finding fresh expressions of church to be an effective means
of evangelizing and ministering to human
needs. It is now, in fact, a multidenominational, multinational movement.

Those of us outside England have the
advantage of learning from our courageous
and creative brothers and sisters there.
England is generally thought to be trend-
ing some years beyond lands like the United
States in the numerical decline of the Christian

faith. So if the spiritual demographics of the United States are soon going to follow those of England, we would do well to pay attention to what God is doing there.

Fresh Expressions US is an emerging Christo-centric movement in North America affirming Trinitarian theology and the ancient creeds of the church. Fresh Expressions is a movement that sees the empowering work of the Spirit in a new era of missional ecumenism—a unity around the mission of God through the Resurrected Son and empowered by the Spirit.

Perhaps it will be helpful to clarify that the Fresh Expressions movement is not synonymous with what is often referred to as the Emergent Church. The two movements are fairly new to the scene, and share many things in common. Fresh Expressions is indeed one of the emerging, burgeoning, missional church movements. Yet, organizationally and culturally, Emergent Church and Fresh Expressions are not the same. Among other distinctions is the intentional affirmation from the Fresh Expressions movement of the critical role established churches play now and will play in the future.

SOME EXAMPLES

There are just about as many kinds of fresh expressions of churches, in about as many microcultures, as you can imagine. Some feature votive candles while others feature chandeliers. A central figure in some is the jazz musician and a central figure in others is the barista. In some the sermon is a monologue and in many it is a dialogue. Some fresh expressions celebrate communion in each meeting under the leadership of a non-ordained person; others wait for communion until an ordained person in their tradition is available.

Some fresh expressions of church involve lots of people, at least one full-time paid staff minister, and a substantial budget. Most, however, are low-profile and require little financial investment. Some begin with a leader who is bivocational, and others are purely volunteer-led.

There are fresh expressions of church among people in recovery and others among community activists. Some fresh expressions of church are based on where people live and others are based on where people work. Some center around a common cause; some center around a common avocation. Some meet in church basements while others meet in homes. There are fresh expressions of church in fitness centers, retirement centers, and community centers. Pubs and coffee shops house lots of fresh expressions. If you can think of a public place, there could be a fresh expression of church there.

KING STREET CHURCH

King Street Church is a beautiful illustration of the Fresh Expressions vision—a wonderful example of the "mixed economy." The story begins with the people of Boone (North Carolina) United Methodist Church who have a heart for downtown Boone. They blessed a new job description for their young missions minister, Luke Edwards, allowing him to begin a new form of church for people highly unlikely ever to come through the Boone UMC doors.

Early on, Luke met a "person of peace" (see Luke 10) in Elizabeth, who "knows everybody." Elizabeth loves Jesus but has been turned off by what she's seen in organized churches. Luke's dream for church immediately resonated with her, and she became his introducer and advisor.

They began by hosting a series of cookouts to which Luke and Elizabeth invited people who hang out in downtown Boone. They provided a place for the downtown crowd to hang out and Luke listened and learned.

Anna is a young lady who is still deeply involved in Boone UMC, but has plugged into King Street Church and is leading a single mom's group. Anna is a wonderful example of someone from the inherited (established) church (Boone UMC) who is part of the original team.

King Street is engaging people at various places on the spiritual journey.

RURAL POWHATAN, VIRGINIA

In rural Powhatan, Virginia, they have launched multiple fresh expressions of church. Joy church is for families with children who have learning disabilities. Deeper Life church meets on Friday afternoons in an apartment building and is made up mainly of internationals who work on Sundays. Various Bible studies in coffee shops have the makings of new forms of church.

Greg LeMaster, the part-time minister of missions at Graceland Baptist Church, oversees these congregations. This is one of many reminders that fresh expressions of church can be launched by smaller churches. It is also a beautiful picture of a church that is willing to invest in people who will probably never attend their worship services or contribute to their budget. They think "kingdom" before they think "my church."

BREAD FELLOWSHIP

Bread Fellowship is a network of five groups, about ninety people in all, in Fort Worth, Texas. They meet in separate venues: three homes, the chapel of a non-profit organization, and a retirement community. There is little structure to Bread Fellowship, but every gathering contains solid Bible study with an open discussion that welcomes all people. In fact, people from other faiths have decided to follow Jesus simply because they were invited into a genuine discussion about him.

CONVERGENCE

In 2006 a congregation near Washington, DC, was in significant decline and courageously willing to consider something rather radical—a restart in a completely new form. Lisa Cole Smith, an actor, director, and seminary student, submitted a proposal for an experimental new church. From that grew Convergence, a fresh expression of church and what Lisa calls the intersection of art, faith, and the human experience.

Their facilities house worship space, a recording studio, an arts studio, a gallery, unique relationships, and one of the most exciting forms of church you ever will see—a union of life, faith, art, and spiritual pilgrims that is nothing less than inspiring.

LIFE CHURCH

Life Church began as meetings for spiritual conversation in people's homes in Newton Aycliffe, United Kingdom. Susan Sadler, leader of Life Church, explained that this fresh expression occurred organically:

> We realised that it was going from a group to a church. And it was a bit of a strange feeling—we're all equipped by God . . . but it was a bit of a challenge in time because who am I to be a church leader? But, looking around, there was no other so you just have to step into that role and be confident that God will provide all that you need.

Within only a year they baptized eleven people. They are reaching people who are far from God. In June 2014 Sadler noted:

> In the last year we've seen our numbers go from eight to nearly one hundred and the majority of them [are] people

[who] have never actually walked into a church before, which is good for us because we didn't want a church that people came from other churches just to experience something new.[6]

TWO MEN AND AN OLD CHURCH

Steve Edwards and Charles Cheek offer us a story of what a fresh expression of church looks like. Steve and Charles look like something of an odd couple. Steve is a white man with a goatee and an earring. Charles is an African American man with the look of an executive manager. Both of them have regular jobs, and both of them have experience doing street ministry. And they are great ministry partners.

Steve is the clergy advisor to some social service agencies in Hampton, Virginia, so he talked them into doing a housing renovation blitz in an underserved area of the city. While that was going on, Steve and Charles started hanging out in the community, building relationships.

In that same community sits Memorial Baptist Church, a 120-year-old church that has declined over the years from an attendance of nine hundred to less than ninety. Its members were aging, its numbers were shrinking, and its facilities were becoming a burden. It's a common scenario.

But this church has a unique, wonderful spirit. They were more than open when Charles and Steve asked about using their fellowship hall for a new form of church.

On Saturday nights Memorial's fellowship hall—a room that has housed many a potluck supper—now houses what Steve and Charles simply call The Neighborhood Café. (Most fresh expressions of church don't work in existing church buildings, but this one does!)

Steve describes the café as a witnessing community. Writing in an e-mail to me he said, "We hope the neighborhood finds us a place of relief, refreshment, entertainment, involvement, belonging, and relationships. . . . We also hope this is a place that Followers would use to establish and build relationships to the point of growing more Followers." In order to make clear that Memorial Baptist Church doesn't see this as a program to pad their own numbers Steve added, "The Café was not established with the focus of filling the pews, but his Kingdom."

A few of the church members come to hang out with people participating in this fresh expression of church meeting in their fellowship hall. There is singing by local folks, food, and a time of simple worship.

Get the picture: two men have a passion for people who are far from God and invest themselves by building relationships in the community. People in the community are likely not to respond to church as it now exists and functions. A church with resources pours itself into a fresh expression of church. And people are connecting with Jesus through a new form of church.

This is just one of many answers, but it's a good answer, to the question, "What is a fresh expression of church?"

What might a fresh expression of church look like where you live? What about a fresh expression of church among grandparents raising grandchildren? A fire department? A retirement community? What about a fresh expression of church among a people bound together by a language other than English? The possibilities are limited only by the capacity of our imaginations and our willingness to respond to the promptings of God's Spirit.

PART 2 WHY START A FRESH EXPRESSION OF CHURCH?

A giant cultural wave has swept the North American church into a brand new world—a pluralistic, complicated, jaded, high-tech, low-touch world. In some ways, a hostile world.

Some church leaders are sitting around like Elijah in 1 Kings 19 lamenting that only they are left. Others are complaining that the good ol' days have passed. Still others, however, are finding new ways of fulfilling the timeless Great Commission.

The Fresh Expressions movement helps existing churches decide against helplessness in the face of change. It's about congregations with a great history deciding to have a great future of kingdom investment.

The Fresh Expressions movement also is encouraging and enabling pioneers—people with an apostolic gifting and a love for God and people—to follow God's call into innovative ventures. The Fresh Expressions movement offers a valuable, viable, and replicable approach to being fishers of people in a rapidly changing society.

FRESH EXPRESSIONS OF CHURCH AND THE BOOK OF ACTS

A look at the book of Acts helps answer the question, "Why plant a fresh expression of church?" For one thing, some have noted that today's Western cultures look more like the world of the early church than has been true in almost two millennia.

And then there is Acts 1:8: "But you will receive power when the Holy Spirit comes on you; and you will be my witnesses in Jerusalem, and in all Judea and Samaria, and to the ends of the earth." Anglican church planters Bob and Mary Hopkins encourage people to consider those pivotal words of Jesus in a new way. What if one were to think of varying distances from the center of the church?

It might look like this:

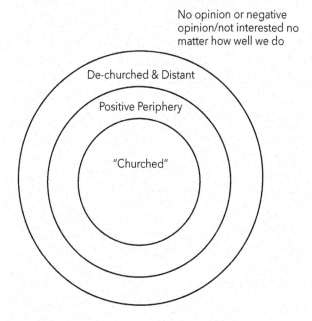

No opinion or negative opinion/not interested no matter how well we do

De-churched & Distant

Positive Periphery

"Churched"

"Jerusalem" here would represent the "churched"—people who are followers of Jesus and serving faithfully in a local congregation. "Judea" would be the "positive periphery"—those who feel positively about the church but simply are not as active as they once were; their attendance is sporadic and support is weak. "Samaria" is the "de-churched and distant"—people who left the church because they were bored, angry, disillusioned, disappointed, hurt, or ashamed. While few of the de-churched and distant ever return to church, some do if there is a crisis in their life, if a new church opens in their neighborhood, or if some other event prompts them to think anew about church.

Beyond the circles is "the ends of the earth," representing the truly "unchurched." These are people who are not at all likely to venture into church gatherings no matter how good the music, sermons, programs, and facilities are. Church is simply not on their radar.

Most churches gain new members from those first three circles: from among those who are already churched and simply moving from one congregation to another; from among those on the positive periphery who have decided to come back to church after a time away; or maybe, *occasionally*, from among those who are de-churched and distant.

Rarely does someone become part of an existing church family from the ends of the earth—those who are truly unchurched. They have either written off church or never have considered church at all.

That is why fresh expressions of church are so important. Fresh expressions help engage those in this latter category, the truly unchurched, who make up a growing percentage of the North American population.

A MODEL OF THE MIXED ECONOMY OF CHURCHES

Chapters 11–15 of Acts tell the story of two congregations: 1) the established, inherited, resourced congregation attracting new Jewish believers in Jerusalem; and 2) the creative, flexible congregation engaging Greeks in Antioch.

Not surprisingly, there were some tensions between the two. (New offshoots of established organizations often cause people some angst.) The people in Jerusalem and Antioch had differing ideas about the importance of Jewish traditions, for example, and probably had differing ideas about how involved the people in Jerusalem should be in Antioch's business.

Yet there was a definite link between the two, and Antioch recognized the value of Jerusalem's blessing and mentorship. There were advocates in Jerusalem for what was going on in Antioch. And the Antioch church connected with unreached people in ways that the Jerusalem church probably never could have.

Jerusalem and Antioch needed each other. The stability and depth of Jerusalem, together with the rather cutting-edge evangelistic ministry of Antioch, provided effective outreach to a world hearing of Jesus for the first time. In those two congregations is found a glimpse into the fresh expressions model—a new form of church coming alongside existing congregations for the sake of those who are not part of any church.

FRESH EXPRESSIONS OF CHURCH ARE ROOTED IN THEOLOGY

Theology, often called the queen of the sciences, had its beginning in mission fields, not academic halls. The Christian faith's most important theologian, the apostle Paul, was first and foremost a missionary. His theological reflections, inspired by God's Spirit, occurred on the front lines of the advance of God's kingdom. The church is always at our best when theology and mission are intertwined and interdependent.

There are two particularly noteworthy theological underpinnings of the Fresh Expressions movement: the Trinity and the incarnation.

THE TRINITY

There is one God. Yet God eternally exists, and has revealed himself, as tri-unity—Father, Son, and Holy Spirit. The mystical and eternal relationship of the Father, Son, and Spirit is a model for his church.

The persons of the Trinity are distinct as persons, yet one in their essence. God is without beginning and without end in a communion unlike anything for which we have human vocabulary or categories. And he—as Father, Son, and Spirit—gives himself to the world and its people. As is so powerfully stated in *The Mission-Shaped Church*, "The communion of the persons of the Trinity is not to be understood as closed in on itself, but rather open in an outgoing movement of generosity. Creation and redemption are the overflow of God's triune life."[1] A fresh expression of church, then, as any church should be, is *in community, on mission.*

We can do the work of Christian mission alongside others much more effectively than we can as isolated individuals. If one is part of a community of Christ-followers with a common calling, engaging people far from God is far less lonesome and discouraging. Moreover, those on the outside looking in can actually see the gospel lived out among people. It's one thing to know a solitary Christ-follower who represents Jesus well. It's another thing—a more effective thing—to see a group of people who actually love each other being church beyond the walls of a sacred building.

THE INCARNATION

The incarnation is God the Son, the second person of the Trinity, becoming flesh. Eugene H. Peterson put John 1:14 this way: "The Word became flesh and blood, and moved into the neighborhood" (MSG). What a deep and wonderful mystery!

It was in the fifth century, at a large council in the Greek city of Chalcedon, that the incarnation was most fully explained (as well as humans can explain such a deep mystery): *Our Lord Jesus Christ . . . truly God and truly man . . . in two natures, without confusion . . . without division, without separation; the distinction of natures being in no way annulled by the union.*[2] Or, in words we are more likely to hear today, as much human as if he were not God, and as much God as if he were not human. In the incarnation, we see the nature of God, and the Christian faith rests on the foundation of the incarnation.

Following Jesus in his mission to the world requires an imitation, even if in small ways, of his "enfleshment." And that means more than inviting people to events at our church buildings.

Here's one way to look at it: imagine a canyon. On one side of the canyon sits a church. On the other side live a large number of people who are far from the church and far from God. The people of the church have at least three options: One, they can do nothing. "If those people want to come, they know where we are," might be the theme of the first option. Sadly, most churches seem to prefer this option.

A second option is to build a bridge across the chasm, walk across that bridge, perform acts of kindness and get to know the people on the other side, then invite them back across the bridge to the church. The good news is that some people will accept the invitation to cross that bridge to the church. The number of people willing to do that, however, is declining. Furthermore, this model extracts people from their context, essentially cutting them off from their networks of relationships with people who are far from God.

But there is at least one more option. An even better option. That is to build a bridge, walk across to the other side, serve the people in meaningful ways, and prayerfully wonder what church might look like among these particular people. Then start new forms (fresh expressions) of church among the people there—churches that spring up naturally, contextually, within that setting and among those particular people. More and more churches are finding this to be their calling—to incarnate the gospel through innovative models—fresh expressions—of church. This is a more incarnational approach.

INDIGENOUS CHURCHES

In 1974, Orlando Costas asked a powerful question: "Can an unevangelized world, caught up in a process of political, social, economic, and cultural awakening, be effectively evangelized by a church that is not indigenous?"[3] The answer was "no" then, and it is a more emphatic "no" today.

"Indigenous" simply means occurring naturally in a particular environment. An indigenous church, then, is one that fits well in its local context.[4] In an indigenous church, everything from discipleship to worship expresses the local culture and reflects the backgrounds and experiences of the participants.

A do-it-like-we've-always-done-it, paternalistic approach to church planting has serious limitations. The roots of the Christian faith go deeper, and the results are more lasting, when an indigenous approach is followed and a church reflects the best of its environment. The Fresh Expressions movement is about starting new forms of church indigenous to their situations—contextualized to fit naturally where they are.

FRESH EXPRESSIONS OF CHURCH AND EXISTING CONGREGATIONS

Individual congregations have histories, personalities, expectations, and traditions. There are only so many changes an existing church can undertake without violating its identity. As much as one might like to think an existing church can reinvent and repurpose itself, the kind of changes required to incarnate the gospel among people who are far from God might be impractical.

Therefore, church leaders can perform a radical church makeover and risk an implosion in the process . . . or a few missional people from within that congregation can begin a fresh expression of church. The latter seems to be a much more feasible option.

When established congregations consider the idea of beginning a fresh expression of church, often one of the first questions raised is this: Is this going to grow our church? That is a legitimate and understandable question. Many churches are not as strong numerically as they once were. People lament the fact that their building is no longer abuzz with activity and echoing with the laughter of children. They love their church and want it to be vibrant.

So, back to the oft-asked question: Will a fresh expression of church result in growth for the long-standing congregation that launches it? The answer: *possibly*. Some who come to faith through the fresh expression of church might end up eventually becoming part of the long-standing congregation. Moreover, some in the greater community might be drawn to the existing church when they hear that the church is so meaningfully involved in mission.

Perhaps God will bless the existing church with new people and greater resources so they can continue to faithfully join him on mission. After all, authors Hugh Halter and Matt Smay declared, "It's a known statistic that the churches that give away, that take risks, that send out, and that sacrificially push their people out, create vacuums that God fills with even more."[5] Alan Hirsh similarly observed, "It seems that when the church engages at the fringes, it almost always brings life to the center."[6]

Starting a fresh expression of church, then, *might* result in growth for the existing congregation. Yet there is certainly no guarantee. Furthermore, the numerical expansion of the existing congregation is not the point.

The Fresh Expressions movement is about the Great Commandment and the Great Commission. A fresh expression of church is a selfless, missional, loving effort to incarnate the love of Jesus in the world.

TAKING CHURCH TO WHERE THE PEOPLE ARE

Have you noticed the *niche-i-fication* of American culture? The world is more divided than ever—segregated into countless subcultures and sodalities. Everything from music genres to cable TV channels has been dividing into smaller and smaller groupings. One-size-fits-all church is perhaps less effective than ever. Taking the good news to where the people are has taken on new meaning. Identifying with people's interests and respecting the complexity of their lives is part of what it means to incarnate the gospel. That's where fresh expressions of church can play a vital role in God's mission of redemption.

Fresh expressions of church allow us to take church to the people. In fact, Chris Backert, the Fresh Expressions US national director, often defines fresh expressions of church as taking the church Jesus loves closer to where the people Jesus loves actually are.

Even when de-churched and unchurched people accept invitations to come to church, they often don't return after that first visit. That could be because much of what happens at church seems so foreign to outsiders and so detached from their daily lives. Fresh expressions of church are about being the people of God *among* those who are beyond the church. That seems to be what most of the early congregations were like—house churches in the middle of families, businesses, and leisure activities.

IT'S WORKING

God is blessing this new approach. In October 2013 helpful data was released in a document titled, "Report on Strand 3b: An Analysis of Fresh Expressions of Church and Church Plants Begun in the Period 1992–2012."[7] This information, gathered over two decades, is encouraging.

The Fresh Expressions movement wasn't named until 2004, and in many ways didn't gain widespread traction for some time after that. But God had begun to raise up these new forms of church in England years earlier. So, after two decades, researchers asked hard questions about the effectiveness of these new forms of church.

They found the impact of fresh expressions of church to be deep and wide. The number of people deciding to follow Jesus, and the percentage of British worshipers participating in a fresh expression of church, are thrilling.

Here are some of the encouraging results noted in that document:

- "It is then striking and notable that in 7 out of 10 cases the growth attributable to fresh expressions of Church attendance more than offsets [the ongoing decline in average worship attendance in the Church of England]." While we cannot yet declare a turnaround for the Church of England, there are genuinely hopeful signs.
- Of all Church of England congregations, about "one in seven to one in eight" now is a fresh expression of church. Furthermore, on a typical week about 10 percent of the people in Anglican churches are in one of these fresh expressions of church.
- "For every one person sent, at least another two and a half are now present. This is a 250% increase over time. There is nothing else in the Church of England that can do anything like this."
- Forty percent of those who are now part of fresh expressions of church were previously not at all part of any congregation.
- Fresh expressions of church have been effective in engaging young people. "On average at the fresh expressions of Church, 41% of the attendees are under 16. This

is significantly higher than in inherited church and is a promising beginning."[8]

The data is in: in England, God is using fresh expressions of church to halt the decline of church attendance and to reach people inherited congregations probably never will reach. Michael Moynagh, a leading Anglican researcher, reflected on the report and declared that, "in terms of outreach and evangelism these new expressions of church must surely be considered our best chance for a renewed impact of the Gospel in the West."[9]

JOINING GOD IN HIS HOLISTIC MISSION

God's mission to the world—a mission in which we have the honor of joining him—is broad and holistic. Biblical Christians are concerned that all persons are treated fairly, since all are the handiwork of the Creator. Biblical Christians will be concerned for the planet in which God obviously delights. Compassionate ministry to those who are hurting, under-resourced, or on the margins is a reflection of our Lord's ministry.

Nothing, however, is more important than joining God in the mission of Jesus, who "came to seek and to save the lost" (Luke 19:10). An intentional effort to help people become followers of Jesus and part of a local body of believers is a necessary and primary element of mission.

These truths of God's holistic mission constitute the why behind fresh expressions of church.

CAN YOUR KIND OF CHURCH CHANGE YOUR KIND OF WORLD?

Rapid and dramatic changes are occurring in our world. More parents are rearing their children alone. More grandparents are rearing their grandchildren. Sons and daughters are living longer with their parents. Families are connecting via social media. People are marrying later and remaining married fewer years.

Drones are patrolling the skies and companies are promising to use them for quick deliveries. There are now more Uber cars than yellow cabs in New York City. People walk down the streets and hallways with their noses in their smart phones. Most of us are so dependent on our GPS that we can no longer find our own way to a new location. People are spending more time at work, despite our time-saving devices. More people work on Sundays. Fewer people are residing in their hometowns. Generation gaps are getting wider and wider. Taboos, values, and morals are in flux.

And then there are the religious trends that began decades ago and seem to be picking up speed. A few churches are getting larger while most are getting smaller. Many people now see Sunday as a family day, not a church day; and fewer people feel guilty about not being in worship. More and more Americans are seemingly interested in spirituality but not Christianity.

Those who grew up in a Christian home and loving church, and those who live in one of those remaining pockets of the country where the cultural expectation is still that people should go to Sunday worship, are the exception; not the rule. Most people do not live in communities where church is the norm and increasing numbers of people have no history with the Christian faith or the church. It's a different world.

Someone once asked, "Can your kind of church change your kind of world?" If you cannot answer with a strong affirmation, don't write off your church. Rather, consider how you and/or your congregation can launch a new form of church to creatively and intentionally engage people who are beyond the reach of your present congregation.

No matter how effective a congregation is, no single church can be everything for everyone. Yet a congregation can use its strengths to begin a fresh expression of church. It doesn't require the entire membership to do that. It just takes a few—a handful of imperfect people responding to a divine call.

A fresh expression of church will become the means by which many can best join God in his mission to the world.

PART 3 HOW DO I START A FRESH EXPRESSION OF CHURCH?

How would one start such a novel kind of church? There are no rigid rules, no inviolable plan, no sacrosanct methodology that pioneers are bound to follow. There are, however, some proven principles that have consistently resulted in communities of faith among otherwise unreached people. But first comes some groundwork.

CULTIVATING A MISSIONAL CULTURE

For many, the first step in starting a fresh expression of church will be to help your congregation turn their attention to the world. Fresh expressions of church can happen naturally when a church has a culture of creative engagement with people beyond their walls.

Pastors and lay leaders can begin laying the groundwork for thinking about fresh expressions of church by helping the people inside the church understand all of the different types of people the church isn't reaching. They can help people inside the church understand God's passionate and holistic mission to the world by encouraging creative, strategic thinking about how to engage those far from God and the church.

Often it is a matter of reminding a congregation of the vision that launched their church or denomination. Remembering the evangelistic passions, courage, and creativity that drove their founders is a wonderful motivation for church members thinking of innovative approaches.

This missional culture, by the way, begins with church leaders and the examples they set. What could you do personally to help "turn over the soil"—to create a missional culture in your church?

FIND THOSE WHO MIGHT JOIN IN THE ADVENTURE

Those called to begin fresh expressions of church will want to pray for others who might provide partnership and support along the way.

There shouldn't be too many church people on the team that starts the fresh expression of church, or else those who are not yet Christians might feel intimidated, and/or the effort might not feel contextual. (These initial teams usually have three to twelve people.)

Potential team members can be invited into conversations, perhaps over a meal or a cup of coffee. These prospective partners-in-ministry are likely from within one congregation, but often individuals from various congregations come together with a common sense of mission to plant one of these new forms of church.

Besides potential members of the launch team, are there people who would be willing to support the launch team in prayer? And is the pastor or other mentor willing to coach and encourage the new team? Both pray-ers and mentors are really helpful.

DECIDING WHOM TO ENGAGE

If you are thinking of starting a fresh expression of church, first think *who*, not *what*. In other words, an initial step in beginning a fresh expression is to decide who it is God is calling us to reach. *Then*, after listening to people and serving them, we consider what discipleship and church might look like in this context.

How does one decide on the *who*? How does one choose the population segment among whom he or she is supposed to incarnate the gospel, live out one's faith, and plant a fresh expression of church? Start by asking these questions:

- Do I, and those around me, sense a drawing toward a particular group of people?
- Am I part of some microculture, such as people who enjoy a particular hobby, or live in a certain place, or share a common interest, or suffer from the same physical struggle? Am I part of a community action

group? A recovery community? Some other group? And do I sense a call to help plant a fresh expression of church in that subculture?

- Do I, or does someone close to me, live in a neighborhood or among a certain segment of the population that has no church, and into which no existing church is likely to move?

These questions, and similar ones, will help you decide among whom God is leading you to plant a fresh expression of church. Then remember: the goal is to do church *with* these people, not *for* them.

The pioneering team should have at least one "insider" in the subculture to which you are called. An insider is someone who belongs to the population group being engaged. If you were to start a church among bikers, for example, you would need a biker on your team. Or, this insider could be a person of peace of whom Jesus spoke in Luke 10, someone in that target community who is drawn to the mission and message, and can open doors and make introductions.[1]

Take the gaming community as an example. Gamers are part of a distinct subculture—people who love video games and/or modern board games. They get together often, play together, share important elements of their lives together, and make up a unique culture-within-the-culture.

A typical congregation would have a difficult time engaging people in that sub-culture. In northern Virginia, however, there are two gamers who love Jesus, and who understand the gospel as well as God's mission to the world. They are passionate about the church and about the gaming community. They are now beginning a fresh expression of church for gamers.

Gamers are but one example. Think of artists, bikers, or surfers. Think of people who live in a particular neighborhood or work in a particular industry. A fresh expression of church engages subcultures like those and just about any other you can think of.

PRAYING

This is a prayer-based movement. So please pray. Pray that God will send out laborers into his harvest. Pray for a vision from God to know among whom you are to begin a new form of church. Pray for persons of peace, people like Elizabeth in the earlier story about King Street Church, who will open doors and provide an ongoing presence among the community to be served.

And wait. Wait until the Spirit says it's time to move. At his ascension Jesus told his friends to wait in Jerusalem for the Holy Spirit. *Then* they would be witnesses (see Acts 1).

When God's Spirit does prompt us to step out, however, it is vital that we courageously obey. There are, almost certainly, more of us dawdling when God says "move" than there are those of us moving out prematurely. The needs of our world demand from us a courageous obedience.

GETTING STARTED

While no one can anticipate or prescribe exactly what others should do in their particular contexts, the following process, roughly in this order (though there is often overlap), has helped guide the development of fresh expressions of church all over the world.

underpinned by prayer, ongoing listening, and relationship with the wider church

LISTENING

A fresh expression of church begins with an agenda no more complicated than loving and listening. Our first act of listening is to God's Spirit. After all, we are simply joining God in his mission and finding our place in it. It is imperative that through spiritual disciplines such as prayer, Bible study, and perhaps fasting, we listen as best we can to hear the voice of the Creator. God does speak, and we can hear him.

Discernment of God's will is a key to fresh expressions of church. God inspired the apostle Paul to write, "Do not be foolish, but understand what the Lord's will is" (Eph. 5:17).

Having heard from God, we then turn to hear from those to whom we are called. Remember the prayer attributed to St. Francis reads, "O Divine Master, Grant that I may not so much seek . . . to be understood as to understand." That is certainly applicable here. We listen to the community—to the people among whom we believe God might be leading us to plant a fresh expression of church—before we start trying to communicate anything.

Asking questions of influencers, community leaders, and business or agency owners can be really helpful. Casual conversations with people on the street, in coffee shops, and even in other churches are invaluable. If you are trying to reach a certain community, study census reports, demographic data, and history. Know as much of the culture as you can.

Instead of assuming what people need or what they think or where they are spiritually, we simply must ask people important questions—questions about their social lives, their common needs, struggles, values, and spirituality. Then we have to listen, *really* listen, before we start something. It is imperative that we not decide what will work before we listen; our strategy should emerge naturally out of what we hear.

LOVING AND SERVING

Michael Moynagh wrote of the advantages of "service first" over "worship first."[2] Those launching a fresh expression of church think of acts of service, not a worship service. Beginning with a worship service has not proven to be very effective in engaging those who have no history with church, see no value for them in the church, or have negative emotions associated with church.

The most effective fresh expressions of church begin where followers of Jesus are genuinely interested in serving the neighborhood or the specific microculture of people they want to reach. That service might be as simple as volunteering for a key group or activity. Or it could mean meeting physical needs if the people among whom we feel called to work are under-resourced.

Don't forget: service usually follows listening. Sometimes we assume we know what people need and later find that we made wrong assumptions. Listening before acting enables us to serve people in meaningful ways.[3]

BUILDING COMMUNITY

As we listen to people and serve them, as we chat over meals and coffee, as we invest ourselves among a new group of people, a sense of community emerges. Relationships develop around meaningful activities. Your initial group (your original team) will begin to expand. Perhaps the people you are meeting will naturally connect with you and your band of missional believers. Perhaps you will verbalize an invitation for new friends to start gathering regularly with your existing circle. Organically, naturally, your community will grow.

As this happens the early stages of a fresh expression of church emerge. It is thrilling to watch God bring togetherness out of what began as casual conversations.

EXPLORING DISCIPLESHIP

We cannot serve people completely unless we discuss, in appropriate ways, important matters of faith. And fresh expressions of church at their best begin with the realization that *making disciples* is the heart of our mission.

As conversations about spiritual issues arise naturally, discipleship—helping people find a deeper and more meaningful relationship with Jesus—has begun. In the early stages this discipleship could be really informal, as in impromptu discussions. With time, planned discussion groups might emerge. Mentoring, intentional conversations, and relationship-based learning are almost always key means of making disciples.

Of course discipleship is more than the dishing out of information. As followers of Jesus live faithful lives in close proximity to not-yet-believers, discipleship happens—a kind of social discipleship occurs.

Eventually, some sort of plan for helping people explore Scripture and the Christian life will be a crucial step toward being church with people. In the beginning, simple Bible studies might help. In some of the Fresh Expressions materials, the following four questions are suggested as a basic and non-threatening approach to Scripture study in groups: *What is the story about? What does it mean to you? What will you do in response to having learned the story? With whom will you share this story?*

This is a stage in the journey that often requires a great deal of patience. "Discipleship is a lot slower than I realized," said one pioneer of a fresh expression of church. We should be deliberate, but we should not try to force people to move more quickly than they are willing or able. Think back to how patient Jesus was with those he called to be his disciples.

CHURCH TAKING SHAPE

As people move closer toward following Jesus they will naturally want to associate with others on the same journey. They might or might not understand how church typically works, but there will be desire for support and mutual learning. Church in some form—church that fits both the context and the biblical principles of church—will emerge. In some sort of rhythm, members of this emerging group will get together and do things that foster their spiritual growth. There might be a small handful of people, or there might be many more.

Lots of people wonder what worship might look like when a fresh expression of church actually begins to take shape. That depends on the people among whom we are doing worship. It's best to think first about biblical principles of worship, not specific practices, so that what emerges fits naturally in the new context.

Begin simply, and check in often with the new members of the circle to see if what you are doing is meaningful. If the fresh expression is engaging people unfamiliar with worship, they will need guidance.

It is important that we be careful not to revert to styles that are comfortable for the already-believers; this is about people who are new to faith. And there is no predetermined model for worship in a fresh expression of church. It might be as simple as reading Psalms, or might involve someone new to the group sharing their musical gifts with everybody.

How to deliver the teaching, or sermon, might be a particularly difficult decision. The Bible certainly prioritizes the proclamation of biblical truths, but in Scripture we find multiple models of proclamation. And the monologue-sermon has probably never been more in question than it is today.

The preacher standing before the congregation delivering a discourse is the form of proclamation most common for most of us. Yet neither the places where many fresh expressions are meeting, nor the people most fresh expressions are engaging, tend to lend themselves to one person on his or her feet talking while everyone sits there quietly. Interaction, dialogue, personal discovery, and flexibility are elements we should consider as we decide on the medium we will choose by which to share biblical truth. The synagogue's blend of teaching and discussion, with the teacher seated, is one possible model.

Of course, we have to be careful here not to let our desire to be relevant and creative rob our fresh expressions of the rich biblical content necessary for good discipleship since "faith comes from hearing the message, and the message is heard through the word about Christ" (Rom. 10:17). We should not ignore the learning styles popularized by such pervasive realities as Google and Wikipedia, but neither should we sacrifice solid content for the sake of coolness.

We are all still learning about effective methods in this new world, so try new methods. Follow Jesus' model of incarnation and explore various approaches to see how best you can communicate divine truth.

DO IT AGAIN

Even in some of the early conversations it will be helpful if you talk about passing it on—about our call to join God in his mission to the world. We want those we engage with the gospel to see themselves as participants in God's ongoing story. Thus we can build into the personality of the group a sense of responsibility for the well-being of their friends, community, and world. Then it will be natural someday for a conversation to arise about the launching of a new faith community. If people have been brought along in the process, they won't know any other way.

In their book *Viral Churches*, Ed Stetzer and Warren Bird wrote about the "Tribbles," furry little creatures on an episode of *Star Trek* that multiplied rapidly because they were born pregnant![4] That is what we're talking about when we say, "Do it again." We're talking about fresh expressions of church that are "born pregnant"—who see themselves from the beginning as people who one day will begin multiple new forms of church.

GETTING ORGANIZED

Someone once said, "A vision without a plan is an illusion." Once the direction of the fresh expression has emerged, it will be helpful to make sure there is the right amount of organization. The goal is just enough structure to provide a way forward without squelching Spirit-led adaptability.

PLANNING

Things might (and most likely will) develop in ways no one can anticipate. It might even get messy! It would be unwise to be rigidly tied to a preconceived design. However, having a sense of direction will prevent the team from chasing every captivating idea that arises.

Begin thinking about sustainability—asking such questions as how long the initial launch team can be counted on for participation and what kind of emotional and spiritual support there will be for them. It will also be helpful to anticipate the methods of discipleship to be used and how decisions about the fresh expression of church will be made. Asking how the new form of church will identify with the wider church, including a potential denomination, will be important as well.[5]

It is critical to remember that this planning is not merely a strategic exercise. The planning phase is a time of *spiritual discernment*—a deliberate attempt to know, as best as finite humans can, the vision God has for you and the place he has for you in his mission to the world. This is far too big for any of us to figure out on our own.

CONSIDERING FINANCES

The amount of money needed could vary tremendously, depending on the kind of new church being considered. For many fresh expressions of church the only money needed is for coffee! Fresh expressions tend to be fairly inexpensive.

So, if this is going to be a cell group in someone's home that's one thing. If it's going to require costs such as rent, upkeep, and other ongoing costs for a facility, however, it's quite another. Leaders might need to consider up front the potential operational costs, sustainability, possible grants, and other funding streams.

Pioneers will also need to consider whether or not they will receive some financial remuneration for ministry in this fresh expression of church. The growing consensus among missiologists, by the way, is that bivocational ministry will be at the leading edge of missional movements in the future. The next generation of great leaders in missional communities like fresh expressions probably will earn their primary living from secular vocations.

AN EXAMPLE: R CHURCH

Following is a story about a fresh expression of church. As you read it, note the various stages we've been studying: 1) Listening; 2) Loving and Serving; 3) Building Community; 4) Exploring Discipleship; and 5) Church Taking Shape. The stages might sometimes seem to overlap, for the steps toward a fresh expression of church are often not sequential.

Matt Senger was a youth minister who sensed a clear call from God to plant a church in his own neighborhood. But this would not be your typical church plant. Matt began by listening to what people in his neighborhood were saying. He explained: "I just started hanging out with people from the neighborhood I already knew. I told them I felt like God wanted me to pull people together to talk about what is going on in the world."

The first thing they did was host a lot of cookouts and neighborhood events. Matt, his wife, and another couple walked the neighborhood and prayed. The four of them met regularly for planning, discipleship, and fellowship.

Matt and friends never hid the fact that they were hoping to start a church, even if it was obvious it wouldn't be your normal, everyday church. For example, one flyer they distributed to publicize a fall cookout read, "We will start with prayer and the Harts will be sharing a short story of faith followed by a reading from the Bible. After that there will be plenty of food for everyone." Not every flyer was so overt. Nor did every event include a faith story and reading from the Bible. Once Matt just said, "Hey, we love you and love God and believe if He were here He'd want you to have a good time. Let's eat!"

Matt's strategy began to shift when he suggested to the original core group, "Let's take these folks we've met at all these big events and make disciples out of them." They decided to have smaller gatherings— dinners in Matt's house—where they would read biblical texts and Matt would talk about them. While fifty to seventy-five still come to the larger gatherings, these dinner-talks draw about twenty-five.

Now a regular group of folks are on their way to Jesus together. A few are reconnecting with church for the first time in a long time. Others have made decisions to follow Jesus and are in the process of expressing it. Several more are still considering that important step. Together they make up R Church. It is a fresh expression of church.

WHERE DO I GO FROM HERE?

If you are a denominational leader, you can encourage those in your influence to consider fresh expressions of church. You might want to contact us at **FreshExpressionsUS.org** to talk about a Vision Day for the churches in your region. Or perhaps you have enough missional-minded church leaders in a particular area to warrant an invitation to one of our team members to come for a round-table discussion about fresh expressions of church.

If you are a theological educator, you have a vital role to play. Your blessing of pioneer ministers and your willingness to help equip them will be a key to the effectiveness of this movement.

If you are an individual who, perhaps along with others in your congregation or area, are sensing a call to plant a fresh expression of church, you would benefit from one of our year-long Pioneer Learning Communities. Those learning experiences cover the basic steps and principles outlined in this book but, of course, with much greater depth.

Please know that the Fresh Expressions US Team is eager to serve you in the fulfillment of your calling to join God in his mission to the world. Our team consists of practitioners and leaders from across many denominations who care deeply for the church and for people who are far from God. It would be our honor to help you.

The kingdom of God needs more pioneering churches, for the expansion of God's kingdom always has been the business of pioneers. And there are indeed some such churches emerging—inherited, established, long-standing churches that are willing to go where few have gone. Those churches are willing to give of themselves for the sake of the kingdom—sending out their best to launch fresh expressions of church.

There also are individuals who are willing to form or join teams launching fresh expressions of church—folks whose passion for people trumps their preferences. There are followers of Jesus who are insiders in subcultures of our world who need a church. There are followers of Jesus willing to live beyond the safe confines of the way it's always been done. The kingdom of God is advanced by just such pioneers.

Do you know such a pioneer? Could that pioneer be you?

NOTES

PART I: A TRANSFORMATIONAL MOVEMENT

1. Alan Hirsch and Dave Ferguson, *On the Verge: A Journey into the Apostolic Future of the Church* (Grand Rapids, MI: Zondervan, 2011), 27–30; Alan Hirsch, *The Forgotten Ways: Reactivating the Missional Church* (Grand Rapids, MI: Brazos Press, 2006), 36; see also Ed Stetzer, *Planting Missional Churches: Planting a Church That's Biblically Sound and Reaching People in Culture* (Nashville, TN: Broadman and Holman Publishers, 2006), 166.
2. For further information, visit https://www .freshexpressions.org.uk/ask/define.
3. Ibid.
4. See Michael Moynagh, *Church for Every Context: An Introduction to Theology and Practice* (London: SCM Press, 2012), xiv–xvi; Michael Moynagh *Being Church, Doing Life: Creating Gospel Communities Where Life*

Happens (Grand Rapids, MI: Monarch Books, 2014), 41.

5. Visit the website at www.freshexpressions.org
.uk/resources/missionshapedchurch to purchase the book *Mission-Shaped Church: Church Planting and Fresh Expressions of Church in a Changing Context.*

6. Visit http://www.freshexpressions.org.uk
/stories/lifechurch/jun14.

PART II: WHY START A FRESH EXPRESSION OF CHURCH?

1. Archbishop's Council on Mission and Public Affairs, *Mission-Shaped Church: Church Planting and Fresh Expressions of Church in a Changing Context* (New York: Seabury, 2010), 85.

2. Visit http://anglicansonline.org/basics
/chalcedon.html.

3. Orlando E. Costas, *The Church and Its Mission: A Shattering Critique from the Third World* (Wheaton, IL: Tyndale House Publishers, 1974), 162.

4. Another word for "indigenous" is "contextualized."

5. Hugh Halter and Matt Smay, *AND: The Gathered and Scattered Church* (Grand Rapids, MI: Zondervan, 2010), 141.

6. Alan Hirsh, *The Forgotten Ways: Reactivating the Missional Church* (Grand Rapids, MI:

Brazos Press, 2006), 30. See also Ed Stetzer and Warren Bird, *Viral Churches: Helping Church Planters Become Movement Makers* (San Francisco: Jossey-Bass, 2010), 49.

7. A summary of this report, *From Anecdote to Evidence,* was released January 2014 and is available at www.churchgrowthresearch .org.uk.

8. Ibid.

9. Michael Moynagh, *Being Church, Doing Life: Creating Gospel Communities Where Life Happens* (Grand Rapids, MI: Monarch Books, 2014), 13–14.

PART III: HOW DO I START A FRESH EXPRESSION OF CHURCH?

1. For an excellent resource on digging deeper into the concept of a person of peace, see Bob and Mary Hopkins, *Evangelism Strategies* (Sheffield, UK: ACPI Books, 2011).

2. Michael Moynagh, *Church for Every Context: An Introduction to Theology and Practice* (London: SCM Press, 2012), 205–10.

3. Two great resources on this point are Robert D. Lupton, *Toxic Charity: How Churches and Charity Hurt Those They Help (And How to Reverse It)* (San Francisco: Harper Collins, 2012); and Steve Corbett, Brian Fikkert, John Perkins, and David Platt, *When Helping Hurts:*

*How to Alleviate Poverty without Hurting
the Poor . . . and Yourself* (Chicago: Moody
Publishers, 2012).

4. Ed Stetzer and Warren Bird, *Viral Churches:
Helping Church Planters Become Movement
Makers* (San Francisco: Jossey-Bass, 2010), 43.

5. Most fresh expressions of church are not
complicated. However, there are some fresh
expressions that require the running of com-
panion businesses, collecting fees besides
regular offerings, and boards. If you anticipate
something more involved than simple gatherings for discussion, you might find helpful a
service like startchurch.com.

FOR FURTHER READING

Archbiship's Council on Mission and Public Affairs. *Mission-Shaped Church: Church Planting and Fresh Expressions of Church in a Changing Context.* New York: Seabury Books, 2009.

Croft, Steven, ed. *Mission-Shaped Questions: Defining Issues for Today's Church.* New York: Seabury Books, 2008.

Goodhew, David, Andrew Roberts, and Michael Volland. *Fresh!: An Introduction to Fresh Expressions of Church and Pioneer Ministry.* London: SCM Press, 2012.

Guder, Darrell L., ed. *Missional Church: A Vision for the Sending of the Church in North America.* Grand Rapids, MI: William B. Eerdmans, 1998.

Moynagh, Michael. *Being Church, Doing Life: Creating Gospel Communities Where Life Happens.* Grand Rapids, MI: Monarch Books, 2014.

————. *Church for Every Context: An Introduction to Theology and Practice.* London: SCM Press, 2012.

Roxburgh, Alan J. *Missional: Joining God in the Neighborhood.* Grand Rapids, MI: Baker Books, 2011.